The
Spice-Box
of
Earth

Also by Leonard Cohen:

THE FAVORITE GAME, *a novel*

LEONARD COHEN

The Spice-Box of Earth

MCCLELLAND AND STEWART LIMITED

TORONTO/MONTREAL

ACKNOWLEDGEMENTS


Canadian Broadcasting Corporation
The Queen's Quarterly
Prism
Saturday Review
Pan-ic
The McGill Chapbook
Tamarack Review

Money from the Canada Council
bought me the time to complete
this and other books.
I wish to thank all those concerned.

0-7710-2210-7

*McClelland and Stewart Limited*
The Canadian Publishers
25 Hollinger Road, Toronto 16

Printed and bound in Canada

# CONTENTS

v

This book

is dedicated

to

the memory

of

my grandmother

MRS LYON COHEN

and to

the memory

of

my grandfather

RABBI SOLOMON KLINITSKY

# A KITE IS A VICTIM

A kite is a victim you are sure of.
You love it because it pulls
gentle enough to call you master,
strong enough to call you fool;
because it lives
like a desperate trained falcon
in the high sweet air,
and you can always haul it down
to tame it in your drawer.

A kite is a fish you have already caught
in a pool where no fish come,
so you play him carefully and long,
and hope he won't give up,
or the wind die down.

A kite is the last poem you've written,
so you give it to the wind,
but you don't let it go
until someone finds you
something else to do.

A kite is a contract of glory
that must be made with the sun,
so you make friends with the field
the river and the wind,
then you pray the whole cold night before,
under the travelling cordless moon,
to make you worthy and lyric and pure.

After the Sabbath prayers
The Baal Shem's butterfly
Followed me down the hill.
Now the Baal Shem is dead
These hundreds of years
And a butterfly ends its life
In three flag-swept days.
So this was a miracle,
Dancing down all these wars and truces
Yellow as a first-day butterfly,
Nothing of time or massacre
In its bright flutter.

Now the sharp stars are in the sky
And I am shivering as I did last night,
And the wind is not warmer
For the yellow butterfly
Folded somewhere on a sticky leaf
And moving like a leaf itself.
And how truly great
A miracle this is, that I,
Who this morning saw the Baal Shem's butterfly
Doing its glory in the sun,
Should spend this night in darkness,
Hands pocketed against the flies and cold.

## GIFT

You tell me that silence
is nearer to peace than poems
but if for my gift
I brought you silence
(for I know silence)
you would say
     *This is not silence*
*this is another poem*
and you would hand it back to me.

The flowers that I left in the ground,
that I did not gather for you,
today I bring them all back,
to let them grow forever,
not in poems or marble,
but where they fell and rotted.

And the ships in their great stalls,
huge and transitory as heroes,
ships I could not captain,
today I bring them back
to let them sail forever,
not in model or ballad,
but where they were wrecked and scuttled.

And the child on whose shoulders I stand,
whose longing I purged
with public, kingly discipline,
today I bring him back
to languish forever,
not in confession or biography,
but where he flourished,
growing sly and hairy.

It is not malice that draws me away,
draws me to renunciation, betrayal:
it is weariness, I go for weariness of thee.
Gold, ivory, flesh, love, God, blood, moon—
I have become the expert of the catalogue.

My body once so familiar with glory,
my body has become a museum:
this part remembered because of someone's mouth,
this because of a hand,
this of wetness, this of heat.

Who owns anything he has not made?
With your beauty I am as uninvolved
as with horses' manes and waterfalls.
This is my last catalogue.
I breathe the breathless
*I love you, I love you*—
and let you move forever.

If it were Spring
        and I killed a man,
I would change him to leaves
and hang him from a tree,

a tree in a grove
        at the edge of a dune,
where small beasts came
to flee the sun.

Wind would make him
        part of song,
and rain would cling
like tiny crystal worlds

upon his branch
        of leaf-green skies,
and he would bear the dance
of fragile bone,

brush of wings
        against his maps of arteries,
and turn up a yellow-stomached flag
to herald the touring storm.

O my victim,
        you would grow your season
as I grew mine,
under the spell of growth,

an instrument
        of the blue sky,
an instrument of the sun,
a palm above the dark, splendid eyes.

What language the city will hear
        because of your death,
anguish explain,
sorrow relieve.

Everywhere I see
        the world waiting you,
the pens raised, walls prepared,
hands hung above the strings and keys.

And come Autumn
        I will spin a net
between your height and earth
to hold your crisp parts.

In the fields and orchards
        it must be turning Spring,
look at the faces
clustered around mine.

And I hear
        the irrefutable argument of hunger
whispered, spoken, shouted,
but never sung.

I will kill a man this week;
        before this week is gone
I will hang him to a tree,
I will see this mercy done.

# THERE ARE SOME MEN

There are some men
who should have mountains
to bear their names to time.

Grave-markers are not high enough
or green,
and sons go far away
to lose the fist
their father's hand will always seem.

I had a friend:
he lived and died in mighty silence
and with dignity,
left no book, son, or lover to mourn.

Nor is this a mourning-song
but only a naming of this mountain
on which I walk,
fragrant, dark, and softly white
under the pale of mist.
I name this mountain after him.

# YOU ALL IN WHITE

Whatever cities are brought down,
I will always bring you poems,
and the fruit of orchards
I pass by.

Strangers in your bed,
excluded by our grief,
listening to sleep-whispering,
will hear their passion beautifully explained,
and weep because they cannot kiss
your distant face.

Lovers of my beloved,
watch how my words put on her lips like clothes,
how they wear her body like a rare shawl.
Fruit is pyramided on the window-sill,
songs flutter against the disappearing wall.

The sky of the city
is washed in the fire
of Lebanese cedar and gold.
In smoky filigree cages
the apes and peacocks fret.
Now the cages do not hold,
in the burning street man and animal
perish in each other's arms,
peacocks drown around the melting throne.

Is it the king
who lies beside you listening?
Is it Solomon or David
or stuttering Charlemagne?
Is that his crown
in the suitcase beside your bed?

When we meet again,
you all in white,
I smelling of orchards,
when we meet–

But now you awaken,
and you are tired of this dream.
Turn toward the sad-eyed man.
He stayed by you all the night.
You will have something
to say to him.

I wonder how many people in this city
live in furnished rooms.
Late at night when I look out at the buildings
I swear I see a face in every window
looking back at me,
and when I turn away
I wonder how many go back to their desks
and write this down.

It is late afternoon.
I have put Beethoven on.
It is foolish to impute pain
to the intense sky
but that is what I have done.
And I will impute loneliness
to the appearing moon.

It is early night.
Down in the lighted city
the tedious hunts begin.
I have been assured
there is no cause for shame.
I am not ashamed.
I turn the music louder.

There's the moon
in my room's window.
I balance it on my thumb
and try to flip it over.
It does not turn,
but still, my thumb
is not broken.
I open the window.
I make the music softer.

I walk on Murray Hill.
The moon needs no legend.
It proclaims its interest
in time, in the immediate night.

I decide to leave it alone.
In my room
the music is turning
because I expect a friend.

An orchard of shore trees
  precise because of autumn
etches its branches
in the grey silk river

The edge of the sky
fills up with blue and soft sand

A barge bearing lights
  like the leaning faces
of motionless immortal sailors
trails behind
  a cat o' nine tails
made of dark chain
punishing the silken water

We never see the river
  run blood red
The yellow sun is lost forever
Its loyal sky
  is crumbling
like a slow avalanche
into its thickening edge
  of soft blue sand

Darkness makes
        a home for the world
The serpents
        rise swanlike from the water
hurl their narrow tongues
at the iron hulks
of the dreaming tethered ships

If there are humans left like me
        along this natural shore
they do not dare cry out
My coat is the colour
        of the ruined sky
my fingers
        of the soft blue sand

## GO BY BROOKS

Go by brooks, love,
Where fish stare,
Go by brooks,
I will pass there.

Go by rivers,
Where eels throng,
Rivers, love,
I won't be long.

Go by oceans,
Where whales sail,
Oceans, love,
I will not fail.

# BEFORE THE STORY

*. . . and from the roof he saw a woman
washing herself.* — SECOND SAMUEL.

Far from the roof,
the child, Absalom,
is storming through
the shadows of the throne,
pausing in the dark
to smoothe his scarlet hair.

And we are lying beneath the thrones . . .

Far from the roof,
the king, David,
begins the ageless psalm
which rings through caves
and tears the cobwebs
from the sleeper's face.

And we are lying beneath the caves . . .

Far from the roof,
the woman,
oh the girl, Bathsheba,
bares her dripping shoulders
in a secret room,
far from any lover,
far from any man.

And we are lying beneath the castles . . .

O far from any roof,
we are lying beneath the castles,
among deep branches of silver,
and the wilderness moon
lives above the whole world,
and in her light
holds us, holds us,
cold and splendid,
in her vast and cloudless night.

Alone the master and the slave embrace.
I will not tell the banker or the doctor.
See, they watch the sun descend
behind the unowned mountain.
They know nothing of covenant or phoenix.
Tonight a sun descends
beautifully behind a mountain,
and my two men
will dream this scene many times
between the times
they punish one another.

# TWELVE O'CLOCK CHANT

Hold me hard light, soft light hold me,
Moonlight in your mountains fold me,
Sunlight in your tall waves scald me,
Ironlight in your wires shield me,
Deathlight in your darkness wield me.

In burlap bags the bankers sew me,
In countries far the merchants sell me,
In icy caves the princes throw me,
In golden rooms the doctors geld me,
In battlefields the hunters rule me.

I will starve till prophets find me,
I will bleed till angels bind me,
Still I sing till churches blind me,
Still I love till cog-wheels wind me.

Hold me hard light, soft light hold me,
Moonlight in your mountains fold me,
Sunlight in your tall waves scald me,
Ironlight in your wires shield me,
Deathlight in your darkness wield me.

## TO A TEACHER

Hurt once and for all into silence.
A long pain ending without a song to prove it.

Who could stand beside you so close to Eden,
when you glinted in every eye the held-high razor,
shivering every ram and son?

And now the silent looney-bin,
where the shadows live in the rafters
like day-weary bats,
until the turning mind, a radar signal,
lures them to exaggerate mountain-size
on the white stone wall
your tiny limp.

How can I leave you in such a house?
Are there no more saints and wizards
to praise their ways with pupils,
no more evil to stun with the slap
of a wet red tongue?

Did you confuse the Messiah in a mirror
and rest because he had finally come?

Let me cry Help beside you, Teacher.
I have entered under this dark roof
as fearlessly as an honoured son
enters his father's house.

# I HAVE NOT LINGERED IN
# EUROPEAN MONASTERIES

I have not lingered in European monasteries
and discovered among the tall grasses tombs of knights
who fell as beautifully as their ballads tell;
I have not parted the grasses
or purposefully left them thatched.

I have not released my mind to wander and wait
in those great distances
between the snowy mountains and the fishermen,
like a moon,
or a shell beneath the moving water.

I have not held my breath
so that I might hear the breathing of God,
or tamed my heartbeat with an exercise,
or starved for visions.
Although I have watched him often
I have not become the heron,
leaving my body on the shore,
and I have not become the luminous trout,
leaving my body in the air.

I have not worshipped wounds and relics,
or combs of iron,
or bodies wrapped and burnt in scrolls.

I have not been unhappy for ten thousand years.
During the day I laugh and during the night I sleep.
My favourite cooks prepare my meals,
my body cleans and repairs itself,
and all my work goes well.

# IT SWINGS, JOCKO

It swings, Jocko,
but we do not want too much flesh in it.
Make it like fifteenth-century prayers,
love with no climax,
constant love,
and passion without flesh.

(Draw those out, Jocko,
like the long snake from Moses' arm;
how he must have screamed
to see a snake come out of him;
no wonder he never felt holy:
We want that scream tonight.)
Lightly, lightly,
I want to be hungry,
hungry for food,
for love, for flesh;
I want my dreams to be of deprivation,
gold thorns being drawn from my temples.
If I am hungry
then I am great,
and I love like the passionate scientist
who knows the sky
is made only of wavelengths.
Now if you want to stand up,
stand up lightly,
we'll lightly march around the city.
I'm behind you, man,
and the streets are spread with chicks and palms,
white branches and summer arms.
We're going through on tiptoe,
like monks before the Virgin's statue.
We built the city,
we drew the water through,
we hang around the rinks,
the bars, the festive halls,
like Breugel's men.
Hungry, hungry.
Come back, Jocko,
bring it all back for the people here,
it's your turn now.

# CREDO

A cloud of grasshoppers
rose from where we loved
and passed before the sun.
    I wondered what farms
they would devour,
what slave people would go free
because of them.
    I thought of pyramids overturned,
of Pharaoh hanging by the feet,
his body smeared—
    Then my love drew me down
to conclude what I had begun.

    Later, clusters of fern apart,
we lay.
    A cloud of grasshoppers
passed between us and the moon,
going the other way,
    each one fat and flying slow,
not hungry for the leaves and ferns
we rested on below.
    The smell that burning cities give
was in the air.

Batallions of the wretched,
wild with holy promises,
soon passed our sleeping place;
    they ran among
the ferns and grass.
    I had two thoughts:
to leave my love
and join their wandering,
join their holiness;
    or take my love
to the city they had fled:
    That impoverished world
of boil-afflicted flesh
and rotting fields
could not tempt us from each other.

    Our ordinary morning lust
claimed my body first
and made me sane.
    I must not betray
the small oasis where we lie,
though only for a time.
    It is good to live between
a ruined house of bondage
and a holy promised land.
    A cloud of grasshoppers
will turn another Pharaoh upside-down;
slaves will build cathedrals
for other slaves to burn.
    It is good to hear
the larvae rumbling underground,
good to learn
the feet of fierce or humble priests
trample out the green.

Sing to fish, embrace the beast,
But don't get up from the pond
With half your body a horse's body
Or wings from your backbone.
Sleep as a man beside the sleeping wolves
Without longing for a special sky
To darken and fur your hands.
Animals, do not kill for the human heart
Which under breasts of scale or flesh will cry.
O swallow, be a heart in the wind's high breast,
River the limbs of the sky with your singing blood.
The dead are beginning to breathe:
I see my father splashing light like a jewel
In the swamp's black mud.

A moth drowned in my urine,
his powdered body finally satin.
My eyes gleamed in the porcelain
like tiny dancing crematoria.

History is on my side, I pleaded,
as the drain drew circles in his wings.
(Had he not been bathed in urine
I'd have rescued him to dry in the wind.)

You have the lovers,
they are nameless, their histories only for each other,
and you have the room, the bed and the windows.
Pretend it is a ritual.
Unfurl the bed, bury the lovers, blacken the windows,
let them live in that house for a generation or two.
No one dares disturb them.
Visitors in the corridor tip-toe past the long closed door,
they listen for sounds, for a moan, for a song:
nothing is heard, not even breathing.
You know they are not dead,
you can feel the presence of their intense love.
Your children grow up, they leave you,
they have become soldiers and riders.
Your mate dies after a life of service.
Who knows you? Who remembers you?
But in your house a ritual is in progress:
it is not finished: it needs more people.
One day the door is opened to the lover's chamber.
The room has become a dense garden,
full of colours, smells, sounds you have never known.
The bed is smooth as a wafer of sunlight,
in the midst of the garden it stands alone.
In the bed the lovers, slowly and deliberately and silently,
perform the act of love.
Their eyes are closed,
as tightly as if heavy coins of flesh lay on them.
Their lips are bruised with new and old bruises.
Her hair and his beard are hopelessly tangled.

When he puts his mouth against her shoulder
she is uncertain whether her shoulder
has given or received the kiss.
All her flesh is like a mouth.
He carries his fingers along her waist
and feels his own waist caressed.
She holds him closer and his own arms tighten around her.
She kisses the hand beside her mouth.
It is his hand or her hand, it hardly matters,
there are so many more kisses.
You stand beside the bed, weeping with happiness,
you carefully peel away the sheets
from the slow-moving bodies.
Your eyes are filled with tears, you barely make out the lovers.
As you undress you sing out, and your voice is magnificent
because now you believe it is the first human voice
heard in that room.
The garments you let fall grow into vines.
You climb into bed and recover the flesh.
You close your eyes and allow them to be sewn shut.
You create an embrace and fall into it.
There is only one moment of pain or doubt
as you wonder how many multitudes are lying beside your body,
but a mouth kisses and a hand soothes the moment away.

# WHEN I UNCOVERED YOUR BODY

When I uncovered your body
I thought shadows fell deceptively,
urging memories of perfect rhyme.
I thought I could bestow beauty
like a benediction and that your half-dark flesh
would answer to the prayer.
I thought I understood your face
because I had seen it painted twice
or a hundred times, or kissed it
when it was carved in stone.

With only a breath, a vague turning,
you uncovered shadows
more deftly than I had flesh,
and the real and violent proportions of your body
made obsolete old treaties of excellence,
measures and poems,
and clamoured with a single challenge of personal beauty,
which cannot be interpreted or praised:
it must be met.

The adulterous wives of Solomon
Lie with young archers behind the filigree doors.
The music from his throne room, music of Negroes
And trained boys, comes over the night,
Past silver doors, into chambers
Where lovers never meant to betray their king.

How they sing, his musicians,
And our friends are lying unclothed,
Marvelling at the beauty of his court,
And though they betray him, these soldiers, these queens,
Why, they are the King's Men, they love and honour him.

O Solomon, call away your spies.
You remember the angels in that garden,
After the man and woman had been expelled,
Lying under the holy trees while their swords burnt out,
And Eve was in some distant branches,
Calling for her lover, and doubled up with pain.

"You are brave," I told the Sleeping Beauty,
"to climb these steps into my home,
  but I regret your man, the Kissing Prince, is gone."
    "You don't understand what story I am from," she said,
"we both know who lives in this garden."
    Still, all those following nights
she never knew to call me Beast or Swan.

For your sake I said I will praise the moon,
tell the colour of the river,
find new words for the agony
and ecstasy of gulls.

Because you are close,     5
everything that men make, observe
or plant is close, is mine:
the gulls slowly writhing, slowly singing
on the spears of wind;
the iron gate above the river;    10
the bridge holding between stone fingers
her cold bright necklace of pearls.

The branches of shore trees,
like trembling charts of rivers,
call the moon for an ally    15
to claim their sharp journeys
out of the dark sky,
but nothing in the sky responds.
The branches only give a sound
to miles of wind.    20

With your body and your speaking
you have spoken for everything,
robbed me of my strangerhood,
made me one
with the root and gull and stone,    25
and because I sleep so near to you
I cannot embrace
or have my private love with them.

You worry that I will leave you.
I will not leave you.    30
Only strangers travel.
Owning everything,
I have nowhere to go.    33

Lower your eyelids
over the water
Join the night
like the trees
you lie under

How many crickets
How many waves
easy after easy
on the one way shore

There are stars
from another view
and a moon
to draw the seaweed through

No one calls the crickets vain
in their time
in their time
No one will call you idle
for dying with the sun

# THE PRIEST SAYS GOODBYE

My love, the song is less than sung
when with your lips you take it from my tongue –
nor can you seize this from erotic grace
and halt it tumbling into commonplace.

No one I know can set the hook
to fix lust in a longing look
where we can read from time to time
the absolute ballet our bodies mime.

Harry can't, his face in Sally's crotch,
nor Tom, who only loves when neighbours watch –
one mistakes the ballet for the chart,
one hopes that gossip will perform like art.

And what of art? When passion dies
friendship hovers round our flesh like flies,
and we name beautiful the smells
that corpses give and immortelles.

I have studied rivers: the waters rush
like eternal fire in Moses' bush.
Some things live with honour. I will see
lust burn like fire in a holy tree.

Do not come with me. When I stand alone
my voice sings out as though I did not own
my throat. Abelard proved how bright could be
the bed between the hermitage and nunnery.

You are beautiful. I will sing beside
rivers where longing Hebrews cried.
As separate exiles we can learn
how desert trees ignite and branches burn.

At certain crossroads we will win
the harvest of our discipline.
Swollen flesh, minds fed on wilderness –
O what a blaze of love our bodies press!

# A POEM TO DETAIN ME

I bound to my temples a box of flesh
filled with holy letters & captured poems –
& I am probably wrong.

With thongs of time
bind to your body
the heart of a man.

I'm heading for another border,
my scrapbook stuffed with murder
& a crazy rumour of glory
whispering through the wires of my spine.

Lucky Cain wandered for one crime
& received on his forehead a sign
which proved in every mirror
who was the slayer and who was the slain.
Blood still is vocal,
the ground is still a home,
but now the voice accuses so many names
I do not know which name is mine.

O you will be listening for music
while I turn on a spit of song;
you will increase your love
while I experiment with pain;
while others amputate their limbs
you will master a ballet-step
away from voluntary gangrene.

Believe nothing of me
except that I felt your beauty
more closely than my own.
I did not see any cities burn,
I heard no promises of endless night,
I felt your beauty
more closely than my own.
Promise me that I will return.

The cage where he ate and slept
Was furnished with gems and flesh
So he would not bruise when he fell
Or his vision ever grow dull.

Garnets are brighter than angels,
He sang as he made his poems.
Garnets are brighter than angels,
He sang as he crushed his loins.

But how he loved the golden feathers
Which fluttered through the cage;
How he loved the golden shadows
When they covered up his face.

If this looks like a poem
I might as well warn you at the beginning
that it's not meant to be one.
I don't want to turn anything into poetry.
I know all about her part in it
but I'm not concerned with that right now.
This is between you and me.
Personally I don't give a damn who led who on:
in fact I wonder if I give a damn at all.
But a man's got to say something.
Anyhow you fed her 5 MacKewan Ales,
took her to your room, put the right records on,
and in an hour or two it was done.
I know all about passion and honour
but unfortunately this had really nothing to do with either:
oh there was passion I'm only too sure
and even a little honour
but the important thing was to cuckold Leonard Cohen.
Hell, I might just as well address this to the both of you:
I haven't time to write anything else.
I've got to say my prayers.
I've got to wait by the window.
I repeat: the important thing was to cuckold Leonard Cohen.
I like that line because it's got my name in it.
What really makes me sick
is that everything goes on as it went before:
I'm still a sort of friend,
I'm still a sort of lover.
But not for long:

that's why I'm telling this to the two of you.
The fact is I'm turning to gold, turning to gold.
It's a long process, they say,
it happens in stages.
This is to inform you that I've already turned to clay.

# MORNING SONG

She dreamed the doctors arrived
And severed her legs at the knee.
This she dreamed on a morning
Of a night she slept beside me.

Now I was not in this dream
Or the cry of the amputee,
Yet she told me this on a morning
Of a night she slept beside me.

You stay in the grove
To ambush the unicorn.
I don't know what the hunters gave,
But all the money of the sun
Falling between the shadows of your face
In yellow coin,
Could not bribe away the scorn
Which fastens up your mouth.

For whom are those hard lips?
The hunters creeping through the green
Beside their iron-collared hounds,
Or that towered head who soon
Will close his eyes
Between your aproned knees?

And when the animal is leashed
To the pomegranate tree,
Don't come by my prison room,
Singing your victory,
Or charm the guards to untie the chains
With which I was bound before the hunt,
When I cried I was a man.

You stay in the grove
To ambush the unicorn.
And after wander to the poisoned stream
Which the unicorn will never clean,
And greet the good beasts thirsting there,
Then follow through the holes and caves
The animals who poisoned it,
And cohabit in each lair.

I don't know what the hunters gave,
But all the money of the sun
Falling between the shadows of your face
In yellow coin,
Could not bribe away the scorn
Which fastens up your mouth.

# THE BOY'S BEAUTY

*For Betty*


I awarded you the boy's beauty.
I gladly dedicated him undiseased and whole
that he might prove the belief in depraved swans,
the tedious theories of celestial assault.
Had your thighs quivered, your nipples hardened properly,
I would not have ordered the mutilation of his face,
the unpanicked dissection of his glory.
But to our relief you honoured with kisses
the thick neck of your husband,
and under the table manoeuvred
his sausage fingers beneath your dress.

Now we include you in all our fantasies,
continue to swear by your legendary flanks.
Our ships from the middle of the ocean,
guided by the sun's gleam on your belly,
resume their commerce between your colossus knees,
and a thousand clumsy poets
lay their stricken heads upon your breasts to sing.

The king's goldsmith once learned to work in flesh
and made his lord
  a toy more precious than his famous golden birds.
Deep in the palace the king remained with her.
Servants, princes starved or went away.
Former guests came once or twice into the banquet-garden
  where now the weeds involved the trees
and hammered figures, and never came again.
Deep in the palace the king remained with her.
He didn't care if sometimes he tasted gold in her mouth
  or cut his aging lips on a jewelled eye.
My love, my love, he sang.
Years they gamed in and out of arches and gold furniture,
he obese and old,
  she lovely as a pendulum.
And when he fell and wept and spit up blood,
on his great abdomen she'd lay her head,
and closing her eyelids like perfect machines,
she'd hum or sing a ballad of their wedding feast.

# DEAD SONG

As I lay dead
In my love-soaked bed,
Angels came to kiss my head.

I caught one gown
And wrestled her down
To be my girl in death town.

She will not fly.
She has promised to die.
What a clever corpse am I!

Call you grass
    call you wind-bent slender grass
say you are full of grace
    and grown by the river
Say what country
    say what river
      say what colour
Tell where is the clock
    in the rose's face
tell where are the speared hands
    bending the fences over
Call you loving in whatever room
    in orchards on seas
knowing not whom you leave
    whom you pass
      who reaches after
Call you falling before a strange ark
    beads and wedding band asunder
knowing not who watches and grieves
    behind his glory wings
Claim you now
    for blood for kingdom for love
Tell the collapsed belly of Mary
    tell the limbs hanging so sadly over
Claim you
Claim you in my father's name
Call you grass

# MY LADY CAN SLEEP

My lady can sleep
Upon a handkerchief
Or if it be Fall
Upon a fallen leaf.

I have seen the hunters
Kneel before her hem –
Even in her sleep
She turns away from them.

The only gift they offer
Is their abiding grief –
I pull out my pockets
For a handkerchief or leaf.

## TRAVEL

Loving you, flesh to flesh, I often thought
Of travelling penniless to some mud throne
Where a master might instruct me how to plot
My life away from pain, to love alone
In the bruiseless embrace of stone and lake.

Lost in the fields of your hair I was never lost
Enough to lose a way I had to take;
Breathless beside your body I could not exhaust
The will that forbid me contract, vow,
Or promise, and often while you slept
I looked in awe beyond your beauty.

                        Now
I know why many men have stopped and wept
Half-way between the loves they leave and seek,
And wondered if travel leads them anywhere –
Horizons keep the soft line of your cheek,
The windy sky's a locket for your hair.

# I HAVE TWO BARS OF SOAP

I have two bars of soap,
the fragrance of almond,
one for you and one for me.
Draw the bath,
we will wash each other.

I have no money,
I murdered the pharmacist.

And here's a jar of oil,
just like in the Bible.
Lie in my arms,
I'll make your flesh glisten.

I have no money,
I murdered the perfumer.

Look through the window
at the shops and people.
Tell me what you desire,
you'll have it by the hour.

I have no money,
I have no money.

Brighter than our sun,
Bright as the window beyond death,
The light in the universe
Cleans the eyes to stone.

They prayed for lives without visions,
Free from visions but not blind.
They could only drone the prayer,
They could not set it down.

And windows persisted,
And the eyes turned stone.
They all had faces like statue Greeks,
Marble and calm.

And what happened to love
In the gleaming universe?
It froze in the heart of God,
Froze on a spear of light.

# CELEBRATION

When you kneel below me
and in both your hands
hold my manhood like a sceptre,

When you wrap your tongue
about the amber jewel   5
and urge my blessing,

I understand those Roman girls
who danced around a shaft of stone
and kissed it till the stone was warm.

Kneel, love, a thousand feet below me,   10
so far I can barely see your mouth and hands
perform the ceremony,

Kneel till I topple to your back
with a groan, like those gods on the roof
that Samson pulled down.   15

As the mist leaves no scar
On the dark green hill,
So my body leaves no scar
On you, nor ever will.

When wind and hawk encounter,
What remains to keep?
So you and I encounter,
Then turn, then fall to sleep.

As many nights endure
Without a moon or star,
So will we endure
When one is gone and far.

## BENEATH MY HANDS

Beneath my hands
your small breasts
are the upturned bellies
of breathing fallen sparrows.

Wherever you move
I hear the sounds of closing wings
of falling wings.

I am speechless
because you have fallen beside me
because your eyelashes
are the spines of tiny fragile animals.

I dread the time
when your mouth
begins to call me hunter.

When you call me close
to tell me
your body is not beautiful
I want to summon
the eyes and hidden mouths
of stone and light and water
to testify against you.

I want them
to surrender before you
the trembling rhyme of your face
from their deep caskets.

When you call me close
to tell me
your body is not beautiful
I want my body and my hands
to be pools
for your looking and laughing.

58

I long to hold some lady
For my love is far away,
And will not come tomorrow
And was not here today.

There is no flesh so perfect
As on my lady's bone,
And yet it seems so distant
When I am all alone:

As though she were a masterpiece
In some castled town,
That pilgrims come to visit
And priests to copy down.

Alas, I cannot travel
To a love I have so deep
Or sleep too close beside
A love I want to keep.

But I long to hold some lady,
For flesh is warm and sweet.
Cold skeletons go marching
Each night beside my feet.

# NOW OF SLEEPING

Under her grandmother's patchwork quilt
a calico bird's-eye view
of crops and boundaries
naming dimly the districts of her body
sleeps my Annie like a perfect lady

Like ages of weightless snow
on tiny oceans filled with light
her eyelids enclose deeply
a shade tree of birthday candles
one for every morning
until the now of sleeping

The small banner of blood
kept and flown by Brother Wind
long after the pierced bird fell down
is like her red mouth
among the squalls of pillow

Bearers of evil fancy
of dark intention and corrupting fashion
who come to rend the quilt
plough the eye and ground the mouth
will contend with mighty Mother Goose
and Farmer Brown and all good stories
of invincible belief
which surround her sleep
like the golden weather of a halo

Well-wishers and her true lover
may stay to watch my Annie
sleeping like a perfect lady
under her grandmother's patchwork quilt
but they must promise to whisper
and to vanish by morning –
all but her one true lover.

# SONG

When with lust I am smitten
To my books I then repair
And read what men have written
Of flesh forbid but fair

But in these saintly stories
Of gleaming thigh and breast
Of sainthood and its glories
Alas I find no rest

For at each body rare
The saintly man disdains
I stare O God I stare
My heart is stained with stains

And casting down the holy tomes
I lead my eyes to where
The naked girls with silver combs
Are combing out their hair

Then each pain my hermits sing
Flies upward like a spark
I live with the mortal ring
Of flesh on flesh in dark

# SONG

I almost went to bed
without remembering
the four white violets
I put in the button-hole
of your green sweater

and how I kissed you then
and you kissed me
shy as though I'd
never been your lover

## FOR ANNE

With Annie gone,
whose eyes to compare
With the morning sun?

Not that I did compare,
But I do compare
Now that she's gone.

# LAST DANCE AT THE FOUR PENNY

Layton, when we dance our freilach
under the ghostly handkerchief,
the miracle rabbis of Prague and Vilna
resume their sawdust thrones,
and angels and men, asleep so long
in the cold palaces of disbelief,
gather in sausage-hung kitchens
to quarrel deliciously and debate
the sounds of the Ineffable Name.

Layton, my friend Lazarovitch,
no Jew was ever lost
while we two dance joyously
in this French province,
cold and oceans west of the temple,
the snow canyoned on the twigs
like forbidden Sabbath manna;
I say no Jew was ever lost
while we weave and billow the handkerchief
into a burning cloud,
measuring all of heaven
with our stitching thumbs.

Reb Israel Lazarovitch,
you no-good Roumanian, you're right!
Who cares whether or not
the Messiah is a Litvak?
As for the cynical,
such as we were yesterday,
let them step with us or rot
in their logical shrouds.
We've raised a bright white flag,
and here's our battered fathers' cup of wine,
and now is music
until morning and the morning prayers
lay us down again,
we who dance so beautifully
though we know that freilachs end.

# SONG FOR ABRAHAM KLEIN

The weary psalmist paused
His instrument beside.
Departed was the Sabbath
And the Sabbath Bride.

The table was decayed,
The candles black and cold.
The bread he sang so beautifully,
That bread was mould.

He turned toward his lute,
Trembling in the night.
He thought he knew no music
To make the morning right.

Abandoned was the Law,
Abandoned the King.
Unaware he took his instrument,
His habit was to sing.

He sang and nothing changed
Though many heard the song.
But soon his face was beautiful
And soon his limbs were strong.

Vincent and Theo
I'll dance with anyone
on your sunny graves
   I'll live in cornfields
under tidal waves
of crowstained sky
   I'll bellow looney sounds
to keep the crows away

   Those who weep for you
who tell tales of tragic art
I'll overwhelm
with jawbones of solid light
   Who wouldn't give his cash
or a lobe of flesh
for six good years of sun
   I'd slice my mind
for half the chance

   O good brothers
your graves recoil like cannon
from the knees
of mournful pilgrims
   Sunbathers
are what you need
with a taste for storms
and none for shelter
   (May your yellow skeletons
be forever happy
chewing sunflower seeds)

## SUMMER HAIKU

*For Frank and Marian Scott*

Silence


and a deeper silence


when the crickets


hesitate

# PRIESTS 1957

Beside the brassworks my uncle grows sad,
discharging men to meet the various crises.
He is disturbed by greatness
and may write a book.

My father died among old sewing machines,
echo of bridges and water in his hand.
I have his leather books now
and startle at each uncut page.

Cousins in the factory are unhappy.
Adjustment is difficult, they are told.
One is consoled with a new Pontiac,
one escapes with Bach and the folk-singers.

Must we find all work prosaic
because our grandfather built an early synagogue?

# OUT OF THE LAND OF HEAVEN

*for Marc Chagall*

Out of the land of heaven
Down comes the warm Sabbath sun
Into the spice-box of earth.
The Queen will make every Jew her lover.
    In a white silk coat
Our rabbi dances up the street,
Wearing our lawns like a green prayer-shawl,
Brandishing houses like silver flags.
    Behind him dance his pupils,
Dancing not so high
And chanting the rabbi's prayer,
But not so sweet.
    And who waits for him
On a throne at the end of the street
But the Sabbath Queen.
    Down go his hands
Into the spice-box of earth,
And there he finds the fragrant sun
For a wedding ring,
And draws her wedding finger through.
    Now back down the street they go,
Dancing higher than the silver flags.
His pupils somewhere have found wives too,
And all are chanting the rabbi's song
And leaping high in the perfumed air.
    Who calls him Rabbi?
Cart-horse and dogs call him Rabbi,
And he tells them:
The Queen makes every Jew her lover.

And gathering on their green lawns
The people call him Rabbi,
And fill their mouths with good bread
And his happy song.

## ABSURD PRAYER

I disdain God's suffering.
Men command sufficient pain.
I'll keep to my tomb
Though the Messiah come.

Though He summon every corpse
To throng the final Throne,
One heap shall remain
Immovable as stone.

The ruins of men and women
Resume their hair and skin
And straightway to the altar-steps
In trembling fear they run.

They wallow in His Glory,
They scramble for his Hem.
These bodies rose from Paradise
But they kneel down in Doom.

Hyenas wait beyond the steps.
I sight them from this hole.
Their appetites are whetted,
They feed on carrion soul.

God, God, God, someone of my family
hated your love with such skill that you sang
to him, your private voice violating
his drum like a lost bee after pollen
in the brain. He gave you his children
opened on a table, and if a ram
ambled in the garden you whispered nothing
about that, nor held his killing hand.

It is no wonder fields and governments
rotted, for soon you gave him all your range,
drove all your love through that sting in his brain.

Nothing can flourish in your absence
except our faith that you are proved through him
who had his mind made mad and honey-combed.

# ISAIAH

*For G.C.S.*


Between the mountains of spices
the cities thrust up pearl domes and filigree spires.
Never before was Jerusalem so beautiful.
    In the sculptured temple how many pilgrims,
lost in the measures of tambourine and lyre,
kneeled before the glory of the ritual?
    Trained in grace the daughters of Zion moved,
not less splendid than the golden statuary,
the bravery of ornaments about their scented feet.
    Government was done in palaces.
Judges, their fortunes found in law,
reclining and cosmopolitan, praised reason.
Commerce like a strong wild garden
    flourished in the street.
The coins were bright, the crest on coins precise,
new ones looked almost wet.

Why did Isaiah rage and cry,
Jerusalem is ruined,
    your cities are burned with fire?

On the fragrant hills of Gilboa
were the shepherds ever calmer,
the sheep fatter, the white wool whiter?
    There were fig trees, cedar, orchards
where men worked in perfume all day long.
New mines as fresh as pomegranates.
    Robbers were gone from the roads,
    the highways were straight.

There were years of wheat against famine.
Enemies? Who has heard of a righteous state
    that has no enemies,
but the young were strong, archers cunning,
    their arrows accurate.

Why then this fool Isaiah,
smelling vaguely of wilderness himself,
why did he shout,
    Your country is desolate?

Now will I sing to my well-beloved
a song of my beloved touching her hair
which is pure metal black
    no rebel prince can change to dross,
of my beloved touching her body
    no false swearer can corrupt,
of my beloved touching her mind
    no faithless counsellor can inflame,
of my beloved touching the mountains of spices
making them beauty instead of burning.

Now plunged in unutterable love
Isaiah wanders, chosen, stumbling
against the sculptured walls which consume
their full age in his embrace and powder
as he goes by. He reels beyond
    the falling dust of spires and domes,
obliterating ritual: the Holy Name, half-spoken,
is lost on the cantor's tongue; their pages barren,
congregations blink, agonized and dumb.
    In the turns of his journey
heavy trees he sleeps under
mature into cinder and crumble:
    whole orchards join the wind
like rising flocks of ravens.
    The rocks go back to water, the water to waste.
And while Isaiah gently hums a sound
to make the guilty country uncondemned,
    all men, truthfully desolate and lonely,
as though witnessing a miracle,
behold in beauty the faces of one another.

# THE GENIUS

For you
I will be a ghetto jew
and dance
and put white stockings
on my twisted limbs
and poison wells
across the town

For you
I will be an apostate jew
and tell the Spanish priest
of the blood vow
in the Talmud
and where the bones
of the child are hid

For you
I will be a banker jew
and bring to ruin
a proud old hunting king
and end his line

For you
I will be a Broadway jew
and cry in theatres
for my mother
and sell bargain goods
beneath the counter

For you
I will be a doctor jew
and search
in all the garbage cans
for foreskins
to sew back again

For you
I will be a Dachau jew
and lie down in lime
with twisted limbs
and bloated pain
no mind can understand

I am one of those who could tell every word the pin went through. Page after page I could imagine the scar in a thousand crowned letters. . . .

The dancing floor of the pin is bereft of angels. The Christians no longer want to debate. Jews have forgotten the best arguments. If I spelled out the Principles of Faith I would be barking on the moon.

I will never be free from this old tyranny: "I believe with a perfect faith. . . ."

Why make trouble? It is better to stutter than sing. Become like the early Moses: dreamless of Pharaoh. Become like Abram: dreamless of a longer name. Become like a weak Rachel: be comforted, not comfortless. . . .

There was a promise to me from a rainbow, there was a covenant with me after a flood drowned all my friends, inundated every field: the ones we had planted with food and the ones we had left untilled.

Who keeps promises except in business? We were not permitted to own land in Russia. Who wants to own land anywhere? I stare dumbfounded at the trees. Montreal trees, New York trees, Kovno trees. I never wanted to own one. I laugh at the scholars in real estate. . . .

Soldiers in close formation. Paratroops in a white Tel Aviv street. Who dares disdain an answer to the ovens? Any answer.

I did not like to see the young men stunted in the Polish ghetto. Their curved backs were not beautiful. Forgive me, it gives me no pleasure to see them in uniform. I do not thrill to the sight of Jewish battalions.

But there is only one choice between ghettos and battalions, between whips and the weariest patriotic arrogance. . . .

I wanted to keep my body free as when it woke up in Eden. I kept it strong. There are commandments.

Erase from my flesh the marks of my own whip. Heal the razor slashes on my arms and throat. Remove the metal clamps from my fingers. Repair the bones I have crushed in the door.

Do not let me lie down with spiders. Do not let me encourage insects against my eyes. Do not let me make my living nest with worms or apply to my stomach the comb of iron or bind my genitals with cord.

It is strange that even now prayer is my natural language. . . .

Night, my old night. The same in every city, beside every lake. It ambushes a thicket of thrushes. It feeds on the houses and fields. It consumes my journals of poems.

The black, the loss of sun: it will always frighten me. It will always lead me to experiment. My journal is filled with combinations. I adjust prayers like the beads of an abacus. . . .

Thou. Reach into the vineyard of arteries for my heart. Eat the fruit of ignorance and share with me the mist and fragrance of dying.

Thou. Your fist in my chest is heavier than any bereavement, heavier than Eden, heavier than the Torah scroll. . . .

The language in which I was trained: spoken in despair of priestliness.

This is not meant for any pulpit, not for men to chant or tell their children. Not beautiful enough.

But perhaps this can suggest a passion. Perhaps this passion could be brought to clarify, make more radiant, the standing Law.

Let judges secretly despair of justice: their verdicts will be more acute. Let generals secretly despair of triumph; killing will be defamed. Let priests secretly despair of faith: their compassion will be true. It is the tension. . . .

My poems and dictionaries were written at night from my desk or from my bed. Let them cry loudly for life at your hand. Let me be purified by their creation. Challenge me with purity.

O break down these walls with music. Purge from my flesh the need to sleep. Give me eyes for your darkness. Give me legs for your mountains. Let me climb to your face with my argument. If I am unprepared, unclean, lead me first to deserts full of jackals and wolves where I will learn what glory or humility the sand can teach, and from beasts the direction of my evil.

I did not wish to dishonour the scrolls with my logic,
or David with my songs. In my work I meant to love you
but my voice dissipated somewhere before your infinite
regions. And when I gazed toward your eyes all the
bristling hills of Judaea intervened.
I played with the idea that I was the Messiah. . . .

> I saw a man gouge out his eye,
> hold it in his fist
> until the nursing sky
> grew round it like a vast and loving face.
> With shafts of light
> I saw him mine his wrist
> until his blood filled out the rest of space
> and settled softly on the world
> like morning mist.

Who could resist such fireworks?

> I wrestled hard in Galilee.
> In the rubbish of pyramids
> and strawless bricks
> I felled my gentle enemy.
> I destroyed his cloak of stars.
> It was an insult to our human flesh,
> worse than scars.

If we could face his work, submit it to annotation. . . .

> You raged before them
> like the dreams of their old-time God.
> You smashed your body
> like tablets of the Law.

You drove them from the temple counters.
Your whip on their loins
was a beginning of trouble.
Your thorns in their hearts
was an end to love.

O come back to our books.
Decorate the Law with human commentary.
Do not invoke a spectacular death.
There is so much to explain –
the miracles obscure your beauty. . . .

Doubting everything that I was made to write. My
dictionaries groaning with lies. Driven back to Genesis.
Doubting where every word began. What saint had
shifted a meaning to illustrate a parable. Even beyond
Genesis, until I stood outside my community, like the
man who took too many steps on Sabbath. Faced a
desolation which was unheroic, unbiblical, no dramatic
beasts.
The real deserts are outside of tradition. . . .

The chimneys are smoking. The little wooden syna-
gogues are filled with men. Perhaps they will stumble
on my books of interpretation, useful to anyone but me.
The white tablecloths – whiter when you spill the
wine. . . .

Desolation means no angels to wrestle. I saw my brothers dance in Poland. Before the final fire I heard them
sing. I could not put away my scholarship or my experi-
ments with blasphemy.

( In Prague their Golem slept.)

Desolation means no ravens, no black symbols. The carcass of the rotting dog cannot speak for you. The ovens have no tongue. The flames thud against the stone roofs. I cannot claim that sound.

Desolation means no comparisons. . . .

"Our needs are so manifold, we dare not declare them."

It is painful to recall a past intensity, to estimate your distance from the Belsen heap, to make your peace with numbers. Just to get up each morning is to make a kind of peace.

It is something to have fled several cities. I am glad that I could run, that I could learn twelve languages, that I escaped conscription with a trick, that borders were only stones in an empty road, that I kept my journal.

Let me refuse solutions, refuse to be comforted. . . .

Tonight the sky is luminous. Roads of cloud repeat themselves like the ribs of some vast skeleton.

The easy gulls seem to embody a doomed conception of the sublime as they wheel and disappear into the darkness of the mountain. They leave the heart, they abandon the heart to the Milky Way, that drunkard's glittering line to a physical god. . . .

Sometimes, when the sky is this bright, it seems that if I could only force myself to stare hard at the black hills I could recover the gulls. It seems that nothing is lost that is not forsaken: The rich old treasures still glow in the sand under the tumbled battlement; wrapped in a starry flag a master-God floats through the firmament like a childless kite.

I will never be free from this tyranny.

A tradition composed of the exuviae of visions. I must resist it. It is like the garbage river through a city: beautiful by day and beautiful by night, but always unfit for bathing.

There were beautiful rules: a way to hear thunder, praise a wise man, watch a rainbow, learn of tragedy.

All my family were priests, from Aaron to my father. It was my honour to close the eyes of my famous teacher.

Prayer makes speech a ceremony. To observe this ritual in the absence of arks, altars, a listening sky: this is a rich discipline.

I stare dumbfounded at the trees. I imagine the scar in a thousand crowned letters. Let me never speak casually.

Inscription for the family spice-box:

> Make my body
> a pomander for worms
> and my soul
> the fragrance of cloves.
>
> Let the spoiled Sabbath
> leave no scent.
> Keep my mouth
> from foul speech.
>
> Lead your priest
> from grave to vineyard.
> Lay him down
> where air is sweet.

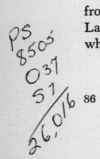